NPL|F
Nashville Public Library | FOUNDATION

*This book given
to the Nashville Public Library
through the generosity of the*
**Dollar General
Literacy Foundation**

DISCARDED

D1379878

THE EXPERIENCE OF ISRAEL: Sights and Cities

VOICES FROM ISRAEL

Gil Zohar

Tower of David
(Jerusalem Citadel)

Mitchell Lane
PUBLISHERS
P.O. Box 196
Hockessin, Delaware 19707

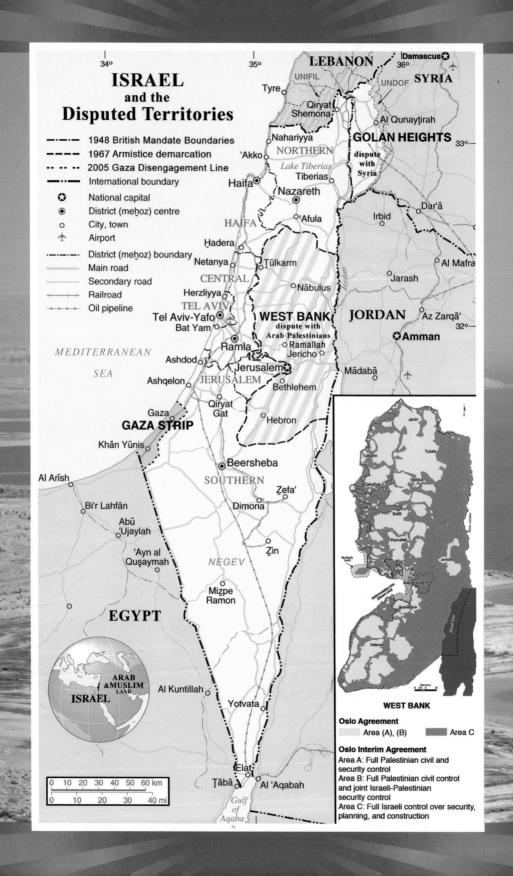

ISRAEL
and the
Disputed Territories

–··–··– 1948 British Mandate Boundaries
–––– 1967 Armistice demarcation
····· 2005 Gaza Disengagement Line
–··–··– International boundary
✪ National capital
◉ District (meḥoz) centre
○ City, town
✈ Airport
–··–··– District (meḥoz) boundary
Main road
Secondary road
+++++ Railroad
····· Oil pipeline

LEBANON
Damascus ✪
SYRIA
UNIFIL
UNDOF
Tyre
Qiryat Shemona
Al Qunayṭirah
GOLAN HEIGHTS
Nahariyya
dispute with Syria
NORTHERN
'Akko
Lake Tiberias
Tiberias
Haifa ◉
Nazareth
HAIFA
Dar'ā
Irbid
Afula
Jarash
Al Mafra
Ḥadera
Netanya
Ṭūlkarm
CENTRAL
Nābulus
Herzliyya
Az Zarqā'
TEL AVIV
WEST BANK
JORDAN
Tel Aviv-Yafo ◉
dispute with
Arab Palestinians
Amman ✪
Bat Yam
Ramla
Ramallah
Jericho
MEDITERRANEAN
SEA
Ashdod ○
Jerusalem
Mādabā
Ashqelon ○
JERUSALEM
Bethlehem
Qiryat Gat
Gaza
Hebron
GAZA STRIP
Khān Yūnis
Al Arīsh
Beersheba
Bi'r Lahfān
SOUTHERN
Zefa'
Abū 'Ujaylah
Dimona
'Ayn al Quṣaymah
Zin
NEGEV
Mizpe Ramon
EGYPT

ARAB & MUSLIM LAND
ISRAEL

Al Kuntillah
Yotvata
Elat
Ṭābā
Al 'Aqabah
Gulf of Aqaba

0 10 20 30 40 50 60 km
0 10 20 30 40 mi

WEST BANK

Oslo Agreement
Area (A), (B)   Area C

Oslo Interim Agreement
Area A: Full Palestinian civil and security control
Area B: Full Palestinian civil control and joint Israeli-Palestinian security control
Area C: Full Israeli control over security, planning, and construction

Jenin
Tulkarm
Tubas
Qalqilya
Nablus
Salfit
Ramallah
No Man's Land
Jericho
East Jerusalem
Bethlehem
Hebron
Dead Sea
River Jordan

Set 1

Benjamin Netanyahu

The Experience of Israel: Sights and Cities

I Am Israeli: The Children of Israel

Returning Home: Journeys to Israel

Working Together: Economy, Technology, and Careers in Israel

Set 2

Americans in the Holy Land

Culture, Customs, and Celebrations in Israel

Israel and the Arab World

Israel: Holy Land to Many

Israel: Stories of Conflict and Resolution, Love and Death

Mitchell Lane
PUBLISHERS

Copyright © 2016 by Mitchell Lane Publishers, Inc. All rights reserved. No part of this book may be reproduced without written permission from the publisher. Printed and bound in the United States of America.

Printing   1   2   3   4   5   6   7   8   9

Library of Congress Cataloging-in-Publication Data
Zohar, Gil, author.
 The experience of Israel : sights and cities / by Gil Zohar.
    pages cm. — (Voices from Israel)
 Includes bibliographical references and index.
 Summary: "Written by an author who lives in Israel, this book gives kids from other parts of the world insight into the sights and cities in Israel today. Kids will learn the history of Israel and famous sites including the Old and new cities of Jerusalem; Lake Kinneret, the Galilee, and the Dead Sea; Caesarea water technology; the environment; birds, beasts, and the Bible; UNESCO's World Heritage sites; and the fun activities available in Eliat"—Provided by publisher.
 ISBN 978-1-61228-682-2 (library bound)
 1. Israel—History—Juvenile literature. I. Title.
 DS126.5.Z64 2015
 956.94—dc23
                                                                                           2015003198

eBook ISBN: 978-1-61228-691-4

DEDICATION: Dedicated to my mother Joyce Raymond and her indomitable spirit. Raised in London, Great Britain, she survived the Luftwaffe's Blitz, and the V1 and V2 rockets during World War II; spent her adult life in Toronto, Canada; and made aliyah (immigrated) to Jerusalem, Israel, in 2014 at the age of 85. Today she volunteers with a canteen for Zahal (Israel Defense Force) soldiers.

"There is hope for your future," says the Lord. "Your children will come again to their own land."—Jeremiah 31:17

ABOUT THE COVER: The Tower of David, also known as the Jerusalem Citadel, was in use for 2,000 years as Jerusalem's fortress. It's likely Pontius Pilate judged Jesus here. Today the site is a museum.

PUBLISHER'S NOTE: This book is based on the author's extensive work as a journalist based in Jerusalem, Israel. Documentation is contained on pp. 60–61.
    The Internet sites referenced herein were active as of the publication date. Due to the fleeting nature of some web sites, we cannot guarantee they will all be active when you are reading this book.
    To reflect current usage, we have chosen to use the secular era designations BCE ("before the common era") and CE ("of the common era") instead of the traditional designations BC ("before Christ") and AD (*anno Domini,* "in the year of the Lord").

PRONUNCIATION NOTE: The author has included pronunciations for many of the Hebrew words in this book. In these pronunciations, the letters "ch" are not pronounced like the "ch" in "children." Instead, the letters "ch" represent the Hebrew letter chet, which sounds like a "kh" or hard "h" sound, similar to the "ch" in "Loch Ness Monster."

PBP

CONTENTS

BOLD words in the text can be found in the glossary.

Introduction

Shalom. That means peace in Hebrew—the *lingua franca* of Israel. And *salaam*. That means peace in Arabic—the main language in the Middle East. Both also mean hello. And goodbye. And they're both written in different alphabets with only consonants and no vowels. From right to left.

Confused? How can one word mean three things? In two languages and two alphabets? In one bilingual country? And written backwards?

Well, that's Israel and that's the Middle East, my part of our world. Sometimes I call it the Muddle East, a chaotic, strife-ridden place where many things have multiple names and meanings, and everyone has a long memory, if not a historical grudge.

For billions of people on Earth who are Jewish, Christian, and Muslim, Israel is the Holy Land. It is the place where much of the Hebrew Bible, the New Testament, and even part of the Quran (Islam's scriptures) took place.

I live in a stone house built in 1886 in downtown Jerusalem, the capital of Israel. There's a looming eucalyptus in my courtyard. An orange tree provides some color. A municipal bylaw requires that all the city's buildings be built with limestone—or at least clad with it. At sunset the stones give off a mellow glow, hence the name Jerusalem of Gold. (I rarely get up for sunrise.)

My home is in the new city's beating heart—the bar district. Saturday nights are pretty noisy—probably just like where you live. Stupid drunken teenagers are the same everywhere in the world. Down the street is McDonald's. But rather than hamburgers, I prefer eating Middle Eastern delicacies like kebab, and *humus* and *falafel* (both made from chickpeas).

While Coca-Cola is the same pretty much everywhere, coffee is different here. American-style java is brewed, but many people savor a fine grind boiled with sugar and cardamom spice. This is Arabic coffee. Or Turkish coffee. Or Greek coffee. Or Armenian coffee. See what I mean about things having multiple names or meanings?

Some no-time-to-waste Israelis just pour boiling water over fine grind coffee and sugar. They call this "mud". Don't finish your cup or you'll get a mouthful of grit.

"YICH-sa," we say in Hebrew. It means gross. It's a guttural CH, like a Scottish "loch." Go ahead. Try to say it—if you can.

My home lies along Jerusalem's gleaming, *ultra-moderne* French-built streetcar with its gravity-defying Bridge of Strings. Most people here hate its modernity. A cluster of skyscrapers under construction form Jerusalem's new business district. Two tram stops away is the historic Old City ringed by five-hundred-year-old Turkish walls. Here are the places where the Holy Temple stood (In Judaism, this is where God resided on Earth), where Jesus was crucified two thousand years ago, and where Muhammad ascended to the seventh heaven seven centuries after that.

You see, in Israel the sacred and the plain are all jumbled together side-by-side. Archaeological ruins of castles can be found here, too, along with ordinary homes thousands of years old. High tech wonders of today's start-up nation jostle beside the two-thousand-year-old **civil engineering** marvels of the Roman world, and extraordinary waterworks from the Bible nearly twice as old as that.

I work as a tour guide here. After studying for two years, and hiking from Dan to Beer Sheba, from snow-covered Mount Hermon and the green forests of the Galilee in the north to the brown Negev Desert in the south and on to the Red Sea, the Israeli government's Ministry of Tourism in Jerusalem issued a professional license to four of the thirty students in my class.

Ouch.

Israel can be a tough place. And the Middle East is a rough neighborhood of ever-shifting alliances where the enemy of my enemy is my friend. Most Israelis, boys and girls, serve in the army for two or three years. The Israel Defense Forces (IDF) is a feisty citizens' army that strikes fear in the hearts of its enemies, and may have an arsenal of nuclear weapons. Everyone has a war story.

I've had rockets fired at me from the Gaza Strip. They missed.

Which is why I'm still doing what I love best—taking people on adventures across Israel, my fascinating home that's the world's biggest tiny country. Both familiar yet exotic, it's a place that's the same size as New Jersey but as varied as the whole of the United States.

Welcome on a journey to eight of my favorite sights and cities. We'll be visiting the cradle of monotheism and extraordinary archaeological and historical sites. And we'll also explore modern Israel—a fast-growing center for global innovation in surprising areas, like drones (unmanned aircraft vehicles) and drip irrigation (a method of watering crops that uses less water).

Shalom from Jerusalem, the Holy City of Peace.

Gil Zohar

The Muristan fountain in the Christian Quarter

The Damascus Gate leading to the Muslim Quarter

The Armenian Quarter

The Cardo (background) in the Jewish Quarter of Jerusalem's Old City. Roman Jerusalem lies buried beneath today's Old City but the geometric division into four quarters has survived. Today they are called the Armenian, Christian, Jewish, and Muslim Quarters. The holy hill called by Jews the Temple Mount and by Muslims the *Haram ash-Sharif* (the Noble Sanctuary) forms a fifth district. Millions of pilgrims and tourists of all faiths flock to Jerusalem's sacred sites, including the Western Wall, Church of the Holy Sepulcher, and the al-Aqsa Mosque.

CHAPTER 1
Jerusalem's Old City

Some forty thousand people today live in Jerusalem's crowded historic walled city.[1] The Old City is roughly one-third of a mile square (one square kilometer), following urban planning of classical Rome.

Archaeologists have revealed sections of the *Cardo*—the north-south main road that was built nearly two thousand years ago. The Cardo was the market heart of a Roman city, lined with shops and pillars.

Like other Roman cities, Jerusalem's main east-west road was called the *Decamanus*. The *Forum*, a public square where people gathered to trade goods and discuss politics, was located at the intersection of the Cardo and the Decamanus. Both the Decamanus and the Forum lie buried under today's alleys, many of which date back one thousand years or more. These alleys reflect the maze-like Arab urban design that can be found in *medinas* (a walled section of a city with narrow streets) across the Middle East. Some sections of the ancient Cardo are open for people to walk on.

The Old City is divided unequally into the Jewish, Christian, Muslim, and Armenian Quarters. While the Old City's seven gates are no longer locked at night, until 150 years ago they were. People were afraid, and the thick walls and towers provided a sense of security. Today security cameras do the same thing.

Friday is the best time to experience Old Jerusalem's unique spiritual atmosphere. In the morning tens of thousands of Muslims stretch out their prayer rugs at the al-Aqsa Mosque. Though the Quran does not mention Jerusalem **explicitly**, it describes a night journey during which the prophet Muhammad traveled to the "farthest mosque." The *hadith* (Islamic teachings) says this mosque is al-Aqsa.[2] Worshippers ritually wash their hands, feet, and face, and turn barefoot to face the **Ka'aba** in Mecca, Saudi Arabia. The spillover line up in neat rows on the holy ground by the octagonal, golden-roofed shrine called the Dome of the Rock.

Alas on Fridays non-Muslims are not permitted to join the prayers or even step inside the sacred buildings. Don't try bringing a Bible or New Testament with you the other days. The strict guards will take it.

In the afternoon Franciscan friars lead a Roman Catholic procession carrying a cross along the Via Dolorosa—Latin for

Jews believe God created the world starting with the Foundation Stone in Jerusalem. Abraham went up here to offer his son Isaac as a sacrifice, and here were built the Jewish people's two ancient Temples. The Western Wall is a remnant of the Second Temple

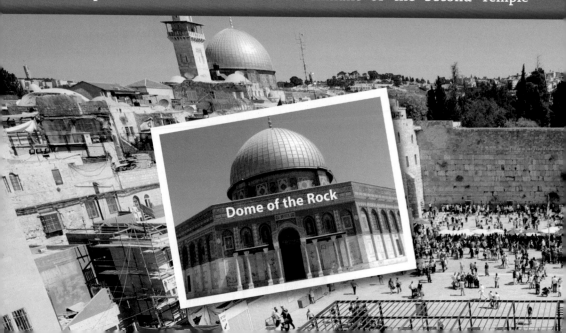

Dome of the Rock

"the way of the sorrows." This street is said to be the path that Jesus walked to his crucifixion. The photogenic pilgrimage winds through the steep alleys to Skull Hill or Golgotha. Here the sprawling Crusader-era (1095–1291 CE) Church of the Holy Sepulcher marks the place where Jesus was crucified, buried, and Christians believe resurrected circa 33 CE. Everyone is welcome to join the pageant.

At sunset, crowds of Jews dressed in their Sabbath silks and fur hats, as well as jeans, assemble at the Western Wall (although the Holy Temple was destroyed in 70 CE, this section of its retaining walls remains.) They've come to greet the once-a-week Sabbath queen with loud song and dance. Look hopeful and there's a good chance you'll get invited home for Sabbath dinner. Think of Santa Claus coming fifty-two times a year. For real, with lots of goodies, like rugelach, sponge cake, fruit compote, and cookies.

complex, where Jesus came on pilgrimage before being crucified. Muslims believe Muhammad ascended to the seventh heaven from this same rock. Today the sacred precinct contains the Dome of the Rock and the al-Aqsa Mosque.

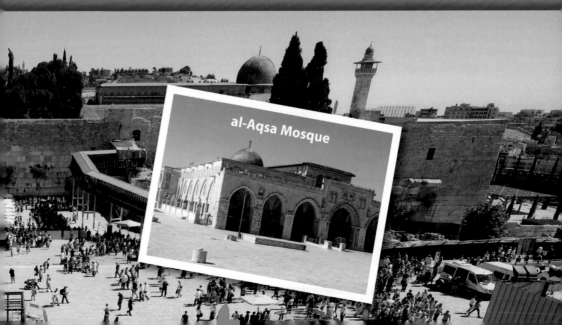

al-Aqsa Mosque

Fridays are holy in Jerusalem. Tens of thousands of Muslims, Christians, and Jews flock to the Old City for the three religions' respective sacred celebrations. Especially photogenic are the Christian pilgrims carrying a heavy cross along the Via Dolorosa. Today the site of Jesus's crucifixion, burial, and resurrection is marked by the Crusader-era Church of the Holy Sepulcher.

What about your camera? Fuhgedaboutit. Put your iPad away during the twenty-five-hour Sabbath, lest you offend worshippers at the Western Wall. For them, photography is a violation of the rules of God's holy day of rest.

While Jerusalem's Jews and Muslims live in the January 1 to December 31 Gregorian (solar) calendar, they also experience time in the rhythm of their respective lunar calendars. Dates vary from year to year because the moon orbits the Earth twelve times in about 354 1/3 days, while the Earth circles the Sun once in about 365 1/4 days. Jews, whether religiously observant or not, close their businesses and restaurants from Friday afternoon until Saturday sunset. Christians do the same on Sunday, and Muslims on Friday.

Confused yet? Jerusalem and neighboring Bethlehem are the only places in the world where Christmas is celebrated three times—Protestants and Catholics celebrate on December 25, Orthodox Christians on January 6, and Armenians on January 19.

THE CITY OF DAVID

While Jerusalem can be divided into the walled Old City and the new city that developed in the last 150 years, the original core is the City of David, immediately to the south of Mount Moriah and the al-Aqsa Mosque. Here beside a life-giving spring called the Gihon ("gusher"), the Canaanites built their walled city some four thousand years ago. By around 1000 BCE, however, a new power had set its sights on Jerusalem. Just like George Washington built a new city centrally located among thirteen colonies, so too Israelite King David wanted a capital to unite his Twelve Tribes.

David had been reigning in Hebron, where the Jewish people's mamas and papas—Sarah, Rebecca, and Leah; and Abraham, Isaac, and Jacob—are buried in a double cave. One thousand years later King Herod built a huge mausoleum on top of the graves of the patriarchs and matriarchs. But the Jewish **patriarchs** and **matriarchs** also figure in the Christian New Testament and the Muslim Quran. In the Middle Eastern tradition of sites having multiple meanings, another seven hundred years later the Muslims turned it into a mosque. The Crusaders turned it into a church. Now the shrine is uneasily shared as a Jewish and Muslim holy place.

The Bible describes how the Jebusites (a tribe of the Canaanites) mocked King David. So secure were they in their strong **ramparts** that they sent the blind and lame to protect their city.[3]

It's a mystery of the Bible how David and his warriors captured the strong fortress. The city's spring was protected by huge towers—which archaeologists have uncovered. The City of David is Israel's biggest dig, and is constantly changing as new discoveries are made. Volunteers are always welcome; other archaeological sites accept volunteers in their summer-only excavation season.

In the late eighth or early seventh century BCE, King Hezekiah decided the massive Jebusite fortifications weren't strong enough. Instead he dug a 1,750-foot- (533-meter-) long tunnel snaking through the hill. This channeled the water from the Gihon Spring to a pool safely inside the city walls. Thus any invading army would have to bring its own water.[4]

Sloshing through that ancient tunnel is another "must-do" in Jerusalem.

Make sure your cell phone has a flashlight app.

City of David

Modern Jerusalem surrounds the historic Old City. The new city is divided into distinct Hebrew-, Arabic-, and Yiddish-speaking areas. The light rail with its iconic Bridge of Stings connects the different parts of the city.

CHAPTER 2
New Jerusalem

Surrounding the Old City is new Jerusalem (population 815,000)[1]—a modern European-style city with office towers, multiplex cinemas, shopping malls, factories, hospitals, universities, libraries, expressways, parks, sports facilities, a zoo, puppet theater, and railroad. Most people live in modern apartment blocks. Buildings erected before 1980 tend not to have elevators. Detached houses with gardens, called villas, are expensive.

Some cities around the world, like Montreal, Canada, or Brussels, Belgium, are divided between populations that speak two different languages. But Jerusalem is unique. Apart from the jumble of the historic Old City, the new city is divided almost equally along language lines into three geographically distinct Hebrew, Arabic, and Yiddish sections.

East Jerusalem speaks Arabic, and most of its residents are Muslim. Jewish West Jerusalem is divided into the Hebrew-speaking main part, and the Hebrew- and Yiddish-speaking ultra-Orthodox section. The latter, sometimes called Meah Shearim (may-AH she-ar-EEM) after one of its oldest neighborhoods, resembles the pre-World War II (1939–1945) villages of Poland and Eastern Europe. These *shtetl* towns were destroyed in the Holocaust. But their ambiance lives on here. Pious Jews continue to live their centuries-old traditions revolving around study of the Hebrew Bible and its encyclopedic commentary called the Talmud.

You're welcome to visit. Note the signs about dressing modestly. Don't try driving here on the Sabbath—or you'll get stoned.

Oy gevalt!—an untranslatable Yiddish expression meaning "Oh no!" or "Awesome!" depending on your intonation (tone of voice).

Jerusalem is the capital of the State of Israel, which gained its independence in 1948 and today has a population of 8.3 million. Like other capital cities such as Washington, DC, London, or Moscow, Jerusalem is home to many government buildings. The Supreme Court, the National Library, and the 120-seat legislature—called the *Knesset* (kuh-NESS-et)—are all in Jerusalem.

Most visitors check out the country's national treasure house, the Israel Museum. Housed in a separate building on the museum's sprawling hilltop campus is the Shrine of the Book. Here are displayed the two-thousand-year-old Dead Sea Scrolls—the world's oldest Bible manuscripts.

The Israel Museum also has one of the world's richest collections of historic Jewish clothing and costumes. This includes wedding gowns from around the world that some would say are to die for.

Four **synagogues**, all centuries old, have been brought here from Germany, Italy, India, and Suriname (in South America) as permanent displays. Together the museum's collections of archaeology, folklore, and Judaica (ritual items like candlesticks and wine cups) tell the story of the Jewish people in Israel in Biblical times, in exile until 1948, and as a reborn country since then.

For many centuries people considered Jerusalem to be the crossroads of the world. A map made in 1581 by the German cartographer Heinrich Bünting depicts Jerusalem as the center

The Dead Sea Scrolls inside the Shrine

The Shrine of the Book at the Israel Museum, Jerusalem

The Dead Sea Scrolls

In 1947, the first of the Dead Sea Scrolls were found in the Qumran Caves (background) near the Dead Sea. A collection of 981 different sectarian religious texts and fragments of the Hebrew Bible were discovered in the area over the next decade. The discoveries proved that the Bible has been accurately preserved for more than two thousand years.

of a clover leaf uniting Europe, Africa, and Asia. Bünting's map inspired a sculpture at Teddy Park near the Old City where children come during the long summer to splash and dance in the musical fountain performance.

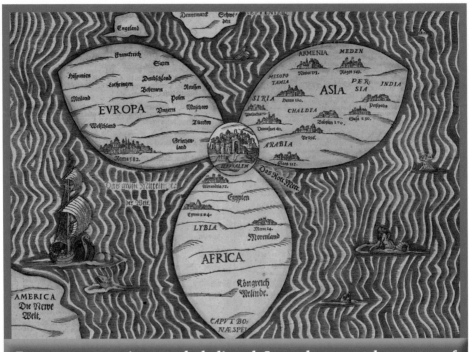

For many centuries people believed Jerusalem was the center of the world. This 1581 map by German cartographer Heinrich Bünting depicts the city uniting Europe, Africa, and Asia. Note the newly-discovered continent of America in the far left corner.

In the late nineteenth and early twentieth centuries many countries lavished projects on Jerusalem. A nation's architectural presence in the city was considered a sign of its power and importance. Thus today Jerusalem is studded with buildings like the Austrian Hospice, Ethiopian Church, and Italian Hospital. My favorite place of these fairytale castles? Notre Dame—where the Pope comes to sup when he's in town. Alas there are no hunchbacks. Or gargoyles.

OSKAR SCHINDLER'S GRAVE
ON TOURISTS' LISTS

Many countries have a narrative in Jerusalem. Germany's story here includes the tomb of Oskar Schindler (1908-1974). As told in the Oscar-winning 1993 movie *Schindler's List*, the hero saved 1,200 European Jews in Nazi-occupied Krakow, Poland, from being murdered in the Holocaust (Nazi Germany's mass-murder of six million Jews). He is buried in the Franciscan cemetery on Mount Zion.

In keeping with an ancient Jewish custom, rocks have been placed atop the simple horizontal tombstone. It is inscribed in Hebrew "A Righteous Among the Nations" and in German "The unforgettable savior of 1,200 persecuted Jews." The word savior has been misspelled.

The cemetery is a United Nations of the dead with grave markers in a dozen languages including English, French, German, and Arabic. It is perched above the Valley of Hinnom, called Gehenna in the New Testament. The Biblical hell, infants were sacrificed there three thousand years ago to the pagan god Moloch. They were thrown live into the fire to make up for their parents' misdeeds, or perhaps to keep the gods from getting angry. According to Arab folklore, one can still hear the victims' screams in the quiet of the night.

Across Jerusalem on a ridge on the western edge of the city stands Yad Vashem, Israel's national Holocaust shrine. In heartbreaking detail, the museum tells multiple stories: of the victims and those who survived; of the perpetrators; of the witnesses and bystanders; and of the rescuers. Schindler has a place of honor there too, on the tree-lined Avenue of the Righteous Among the Nations. His is one of 25,271 carefully documented cases of people who risked life and limb during World War II to save Jews.[2]

Sulaiman Abu Zayad, a Palestinian peasant from the nearby village of al-Azariyya—where Jesus resurrected Lazarus from among the dead—has been keeping his lonely vigil on Mount Zion for half a century. He clearly remembers digging Schindler's grave decades ago and burying him.

How is it, I ask Abu Zayad, that a Muslim is in charge of a Catholic cemetery where a non-believer is buried who saved 1,200 Jews? *"Nihna kulna bani Allah"* (We are all the children of God), he responds.[3]

Tel Aviv today is a bustling metropolis, and the heart of Israel. Founded on sand dunes in 1909, the seaside city has grown to include the stock market and the main offices of many corporations, as well as the Ministry of Defense and the Mossad spy department.

CHAPTER 3
SHOW AND TEL—
The Big Orange is
Israel's Business Heart

If Jerusalem is ageless, Tel Aviv—the multicultural metropolis called by some the Big Orange—is barely a century old. The two cities, linked by an expressway and a high-speed twenty-nine-minute train under construction, are as different as imaginable.

Jerusalem is a poor, mountainous city with many students of religion who ponder the meaning of life; Tel Aviv is a wealthy, flat seaside city where people take nothing seriously except their pleasure. Here in this metropolis of 427,000[1] are headquartered Israel's stock market, insurance companies and big business, as well as the Ministry of Defense and the Mossad—the government spy department.

Flanking Tel Aviv on the north, east, and south is an urban and suburban sprawl of satellite cities. This wider area, called Gush Dan, is home to more than two-fifths of Israel's population. The Hebrew name evokes the tribe of Dan who were driven out of here by the Philistines three thousand years ago. They found refuge by one of the sources of the Jordan River at Dan on Israel's northern border with Lebanon.

Today, driving north from Tel Aviv, one sees office parks for multinational corporations like Intel, Microsoft, IBM, Dell, Motorola, and more. This is Silicon Wadi—Israel's collection of high-tech businesses whose breakthroughs have revolutionized computers and cell phones.

While Jerusalem echoes the Bible and the ancient world, Tel Aviv is all about the future.

During Passover 1909, Tel Aviv's sixty founding families met on the sand dunes north of the ancient port of Jaffa—where the prophet Jonah sailed from and was swallowed by a whale. (Actually it was a big fish.) The homesteaders were parceling out the twelve acres they had bought from Bedouin (Beh-doe-WIN) tribesmen a year before. According to legend, the group's leader Akiva Aryeh Weiss, went to the beach on the morning of the lottery and collected 120 seashells, half of them white and half of them grey. He wrote the members' names on the white shells and the plot numbers on the grey ones. A boy drew names from one box while a girl drew plot numbers from the other.

While Israel's version of the Plymouth Rock makes a lovely story, the historical truth is less heroic. Weiss and Tel Aviv's founding mayor Meir Dizengoff were bitter rivals.

That squabble set the tone for a century of scandal and even assassination in what is otherwise a very safe city. The most recent was the gunning down of Israeli Prime Minister Yitzhak Rabin at a peace rally in front of City Hall in 1995. The assassin was an extremist nationalist who opposed Rabin's negotiations to establish the

Prime Minister Yitzhak Rabin won the 1994 Nobel Peace Prize for his role in the historic 1993 Oslo Accords—which promised peace between Israel and its Palestinian neighbors.

State of Palestine on disputed land Israel has controlled since the 1967 Six-Day War. Alas not everyone agrees to give peace a chance.

The on-again, off-again negotiations between Israel and its Palestinian neighbors remain deadlocked at the time of this writing. Elections were held in March 2015. Although Prime Minister Benjamin Netanyahu was re-elected and formed another right-wing government, with a new coalition comes another chance for a peace breakthrough. Politics can change very quickly in the Middle East.

The pioneering homesteaders of 1909 debated what to call their garden suburb. They settled on Tel Aviv, a silky Hebrew translation of Zionist visionary Theodor Herzl's German-language book *Altneuland* ("Old New Land"). Unbeknownst to the settlers, the name—combining the Hebrew words for an archaeological mound and springtime—was mentioned in the Bible.[2]

That irreligiosity characterizes Tel Aviv—a **secular** yet intensely Jewish city where the beaches are packed on Rosh Hashanah (Jewish New Year), and where the car-free deserted streets are taken over on Yom Kippur (the Day of Atonement) by bicyclists.

Tel Aviv on Yom Kippur

Tel Aviv beach

Tel Aviv is also called the White City. It has the world's largest assemblage of Bauhaus-style buildings. They were created in the 1930s and 1940s by Polish and German immigrants and refugees, and architects fleeing Nazi Germany where the modernist International Style was despised by the government. Those low-rise, relentlessly geometric residential buildings, unadorned except for curving balconies, "thermometer" stairwells, and porthole windows, boasted airy apartments designed to promote a lifestyle that was healthy and, above all, modern. It was a revolution in design that embraced the future rather than the architecture and culture of the past.

Think of the fictional but dazzling Emerald City in *The Wizard of Oz*. Tel Aviv quickly developed into a blindingly white seaside jewel. But from Bauhaus promise, the ever-expanding city quickly skidded into the architectural doghouse. Following the outbreak of World War II in 1939, rent prices began to

A modern Bauhaus building on Ben Yehuda Street in the White City heritage district Tel Aviv.

Porthole window

Curving balconies

"Thermometer" staircase

increase quickly. In response, the British government (which was in control of the land, then called Mandatory Palestine) placed limits on the rent that owners could charge. Landlords, unable to turn a profit from their newly-built apartment blocks, stopped all upkeep. Neglect, coupled with salty sea breezes, caused the beautiful streamlined White City to deteriorate into a gray urban dump.

Yet Tel Aviv's defining days were still ahead, even as the decay was spreading. The high point of Zionism (the movement to establish and build a Jewish state in the Jewish people's Biblical homeland) came on May 14, 1948. That Friday in the late afternoon before the Sabbath, the brand-new country's leadership gathered at the Tel Aviv Museum—formerly the villa of Meir Dizengoff. Many wept as David Ben-Gurion—Israel's George Washington—proclaimed independence in the waning hours of the British Mandate of Palestine.

Crowds came downtown to dance and celebrate into the night. Today the once-chic Allenby Street—named after the British general who drove out the Turks in 1917 during World War I—has become run down. During the decline, those Tel Avivis who could abandoned the city center for distant suburbs.

The downward spiral hit bottom as Tel Aviv was celebrating its fiftieth year. The landmark Herzliya Gymnasium was torn down to make room for the Shalom Meir tower. At thirty-four stories, the tower was the tallest building in the Middle East and Tel Aviv's first skyscraper. Today it is dwarfed by more modern highrises. (Israel's tallest building is the sixty-eight-floor Moshe Aviv Tower in neighboring Ramat Gan.) The destruction of the high school landmark sparked the conservation movement to preserve heritage buildings.

In recent decades, the White City's charm has begun to return. Today "The City That Never Sleeps" is Israel's economic,

The tallest building in Israel, the Moshe Aviv Tower (right), stands in Ramat Gan in the Tel Aviv District.

commercial, and cultural heart. It claims Israel's most robust skyline.

Meir Dizengoff, who used to inspect his new town on horseback, would be astonished by today's prosperity. But one thing Dizengoff would recognize—a spanking new statue of himself on horseback unveiled for Tel Aviv's centennial, saluting the birthplace of modern Israel.

Meir Dizengoff statue

UNESCO WORLD HERITAGE SITES IN ISRAEL

Since Israel signed the World Heritage Convention in 1999, UNESCO (United Nations Educational, Scientific, and Cultural Organization) has placed eight Israeli sites on its World Heritage List. This list is considered to be the most important registry of landmarks of human civilization.

- In 2001 the fortress of Masada, built by King Herod as a desert palace and then used by Jewish rebels as their last stand against the Roman Empire in 73 CE, became the first site in Israel to make it onto the list.
- Acre's Old City was also inscribed that year. Beneath the walled city's eighteenth- and nineteenth-century Ottoman ramparts are the remains of the world's best-preserved Crusader city, dating from 1104 to 1291.
- The "White City of Tel Aviv" was inscribed in 2003, for its collection of four thousand Bauhaus or International Style structures dating from the 1930s and 1940s.
- The historic cities of Megiddo, Hazor, and Beer Sheba were inscribed in 2005. The ruins of these Biblical cities contain elaborate underground water-storage systems dating back to the Iron Age.
- The "Incense Route—Desert Cities in the Negev," also inscribed in 2005, includes four **Nabatean** towns which prospered from the third century BCE until the end of the second century CE. These towns linked the spice route from today's Yemen to the port of Gaza on the Mediterranean. From there precious fragrances (like frankincense and myrrh) were shipped to Rome. (The "Eternal City" must have really stunk if they needed so much **incense** to mask the odor.)
- "Baha'i Holy Places in Haifa and the Western Galilee" were inscribed in 2008, recognizing the Baha'i faith's two holiest sites.
- The Mount Carmel caves, where both Neanderthal man and early *Homo sapiens* spent time, were added to the list in 2012.
- Beit Guvrin-Maresha National Park, a vast cave complex located in the Judean Hills southwest of Jerusalem was added to the list in 2014. UNESCO calls this network of underground chambers, which dates back as far as the eighth century BCE, a "city under a city."

Jesus spent three years living by the northwest shore of Lake Kinneret, also called the Sea of Galilee. At the Mount of Beatitudes he delivered his Sermon on the Mount. Today's octagonal church, completed in 1938, reflects the eight themes of his sermon, considered one of Jesus's key teachings.

CHAPTER 4
Lake Kinneret and the Galilee

Tiny, semi-arid Israel has only one natural freshwater lake—but she's a beauty. The Kinneret, meaning the harp-shaped body of water, also called the Sea of Galilee, is arguably the most famous lake in the world. It's certainly serene, even mystical.

Here, at the ancient fisherman's town of Capernaum on the lake's northwest edge, Jesus lived and preached for three years after leaving his home in Nazareth, a village in the mountains of the Galilee to the west. Here he is said to have walked on the water. A story? Or a miracle?

Many churches and religious institutions around the lake celebrate that time in Jesus's mission. At Tabgha, German Benedictine monks have rebuilt the 1,650-year-old Byzantine church marking where Jesus performed another miracle, feeding five thousand people with five loaves of bread and two fish—and having leftovers.[1] Tilapia, also called St. Peter's fish, is a favorite food in the area. Watch out for the bones.

Nearby is Mount of Beatitudes where Jesus preached his Sermon on the Mount. "Blessed are the meek, for they shall inherit the earth."[2]

Christian pilgrims flock to these well-maintained sites and their meditation gardens. Some hike the Gospel Trail, linking Nazareth to the lakeside holy sites. It's best to hit the trail in the winter when the weather is pleasant. Check the rain forecast first. Located 700 feet (213 meters) below sea level, the area around Lake Kinneret is torrid in the summer. Think of Arizona,

Lake Kinneret (the Sea of Galilee) is the lowest freshwater lake on Earth and the second-lowest lake overall (after the Dead Sea). The lake is fed from snow melting on Mount Hermon, a number of streams that join to form the Jordan River, and underground springs. Today the Jordan River at the south end of the lake is dammed. Lake water is pumped through Israel's National Water Carrier south to Tel Aviv and the Negev Desert. Under Israel's 1994 peace treaty with Jordan, Israel also provides fresh water to its neighbor to the east.

This statue of Saint Peter can be found in the town of Capernaum, at the northwest edge of Lake Kinneret. Today a Catholic church stands on the ruins of Peter's home. Originally named Simon, he became known as Peter (from the Greek word for rock) when Jesus told him that he was the rock upon which he would build his church.

with temperatures of more than 100 degrees Fahrenheit (37 degrees Celsius)—in the shade. If you can find any.

Israel strictly regulates development on the banks of Lake Kinneret. Apart from the sleepy city of Tiberias, most of the waterfront is preserved as beaches and wetlands. Crowds of people come from Tel Aviv and elsewhere every weekend to camp out and have barbecues. Be warned—Israelis like loud music. "Born to party, forced to work," could be the motto for many of these weekend holidaymakers.

Israel has a Mediterranean climate, meaning a long dry summer and a short rainy winter. Lake Kinneret's level fluctuates from year to year depending on the rain clouds.[3] Rain is a national concern, even an obsession. Heaven help us if there is a drought and the rains fail to arrive.

In 1964 Israel inaugurated the National Water Carrier. Huge pumps near Tabgha, protected by a massive concrete dome, pump fresh water up from the lake and send it south through canals and pipes to the parched Negev Desert.

Israel's population has grown ten-fold since independence in 1948. The National Water Carrier, inaugurated in 1964, can no longer supply enough water for the parched country. To solve this problem, Israel has built many water desalination plants, which turn salt water into fresh water.

National Water Carrier
pumping station

THE JESUS BOAT

In 1986 a drought exposed vast areas along the shore of Lake Kinneret. Wannabe archaeologists Moshe and Yuval Lufan, brothers from **Kibbutz** Ginosar, set out to explore the land that was previously underwater. They discovered the newly-exposed hulk of an ancient ship.

But what to do? The water-soaked wood was like cardboard. A huge conservation effort was made by Israel Antiquities Authority experts who built a preservation lab on shore, wrapped the fragile fishing boat in foam, and floated it to the special tank they had created. For seven years, the waterlogged wood was chemically treated until it was stabilized. Today the vessel, which some people call the Jesus Boat, is displayed at a museum at the kibbutz "floating on a wave of glass."

Made of cedar wood and measuring 27 feet (8.2 meters)[4] from bow to stern, the boat is about two thousand years old.[5] It was of great value to some fishermen then—when it became damaged, they just kept fixing it. It was their livelihood.

So what happened? No one knows for sure. Perhaps the vessel simply wore out. The winters here can get nasty, so it could have sunk in a storm. Or it may have been destroyed in 66 CE during the naval battle between Jewish rebels and the Romans.

No one claims Jesus sailed on this very boat. But fishing was a common profession in his time. He was certainly familiar with this very kind of craft and the nets its fishermen used.

Masada is a fortress and desert palace built by King Herod two thousand years ago. It overlooks the Dead Sea in the remote Judean Desert. It was here in 73 CE that Jewish rebels made their last stand against the Roman Empire. According to the historian Josephus Flavius, 960 rebels and their families committed suicide to avoid falling into the hands of the Romans.

CHAPTER 5
CAESAREA—
Cutting Edge Water Technology

King Herod (ca. 74/73 BCE–4 BCE) had an identity crisis; half Jewish and half Arab, he was completely Roman. His kingdom of Judea was under Roman control, but Herod was on good terms with Augustus Caesar, the emperor in Rome. He was given the freedom to rule his people, as long as he remained loyal. Herod the Great built huge projects across the Mediterranean world. He also donated large sums of money so that the ancient Olympic Games could continue to be held every four years in Greece.

Herod's construction projects transformed Israel two thousand years ago. He built or rebuilt numerous desert palaces in today's Israel and Jordan, the Holy Temple in Jerusalem, and whole new Roman cities. Amongst these, his most ambitious project was Caesarea Maritima. The *chutzpah* of his vision was breathtaking. Herod's engineers constructed large wooden frames and towed them out to sea, where they were positioned by divers. Filled with cement from Mount Vesuvius, near Naples, Italy, they formed a vast artificial harbor jutting out from the shoreline. Warehouses and an elaborate lighthouse adorned the piers while a brand-new city arose on the land. The Romans for all their ingenuity were poor sailors; wintering here and waiting for the storms to end, boats set off from Caesarea to bring grain from Egypt, the empire's breadbasket, to Rome. The first captain to dock in Rome in the spring received a major cash honor. And every boat paid Herod dock fees.[1]

The ancient port can be explored on land or by scuba diving in the underwater national park. Archaeologists today are continuing to excavate. So far they've shown Caesarea included all the luxuries a king could desire—a hippodrome

The ruins of Caesarea

Public bathhouse

(chariot racetrack), gladiator arena, theater, bathhouses, fountains, and pagan temples.

Herod's palace protruded out into the sea. It contained a swimming pool—in the middle of the salty Mediterranean—filled with fresh water.

Caesarea's Roman theater remains a popular concert site

But where was that drinking water to come from? No problem for Herod—who ordered an aqueduct be built connecting the beach to the springs at Shuni four miles (seven kilometers) away.

In 6 CE Caesarea became the capital of Roman Judea. The prefect (Roman governor) Pontius Pilate lived in Herod's seaside palace from 26 to 36 CE. The Apostle Paul was imprisoned in Caesarea's jail for two years before being shipped off to Rome to stand trial for having encouraged riots in Jerusalem.[2]

Herod's city by the sea and its artificial harbor were built using very advanced technology. Unfortunately, the king's engineers couldn't have anticipated the environmental consequences of this technology over many centuries. Because the flow of the sea had been disrupted, the harbor slowly collected sand drifting north from the Nile River delta. The changed wave patterns eroded a new bay, collapsing a section of the aqueduct.[3] More ruinously an earthquake in 115 CE unleashed a killer tsunami.[4]

But Caesarea was rebuilt, and remained an important city until it was finally captured by the Mamluk leader Baybars in 1265. After the Crusaders were driven out, the city lay abandoned until 1291. That year the Mamluks destroyed Caesarea and all of the former Crusader coastal forts in order to discourage the Franks (Europeans) from mounting another crusade. In an act of tremendous ecological damage, ancient oak forests were cut down. The trees were packed into the castles and set on fire. The tremendous heat caused the walls to crack and collapse.[5] King Herod's dream was finally over.

KIBBUTZ MA'AGAN MICHAEL—A BARREN HILL TURNED INTO A GARDEN

Just north of Caesarea along the beach lies Kibbutz Ma'agan Michael. The kibbutz (plural kibbutzim), meaning "ingathering" in Hebrew, is a unique Israeli social invention—today a cross between a gated community in America and a **utopian commune**.

Degania, the first kibbutz, was founded in 1909. With limited money, the pioneers created a revolutionary society in which members worked equally, men and women alike. And there was lots of work to be done. Members shared clothes, and practically everything else. Children were raised in a dormitory to allow the adults to get the most possible amount of work done.

Though never large in number, kibbutz members played a major role in establishing and defending Israel. Many kibbutzim were built in isolated places to secure the borders. The sites were ill-suited. The pioneers frequently had to overcome malaria by draining swamps.

Kibbutz Ma'agan Michael, founded in 1949 on a treeless hill, fits this pattern. The original two hundred settlers, fifty of whom were children, began with a few basic wooden huts.[6] Draining the Kabarra Swamp, they channeled water into fishponds. The remaining wetland was transformed into rich agricultural fields.

Today Ma'agan Michael has grown into the country's largest kibbutz, with 1,412 members.[7] Ma'agan Michael operates a major **agro-industrial** complex with global exports—a huge jump from its modest beginnings with a single cow, some sheep, and a few chickens.

Prosperity made the original communal nature of the kibbutzim less popular. Children today grow up in their parents' home in all of Israel's 256 kibbutzim. Similarly most kibbutz members, of whom there are approximately 106,000,[8] cook their own meals rather than eat in a communal dining hall. They pay for the food they consume.

The majority of kibbutzim have abandoned the last trace of socialism—equal salaries regardless of the job. Members are free to work where they choose, and earn according to their skills. Other kibbutzim remain committed to the communal ideal of sharing wealth.

Kibbutz in Israel

Haifa's oil refinery once served Britain's Royal Navy, refining petroleum pumped from Iraq. Following Israel's independence, Arab countries began an economic boycott of the new nation. Today Israel is moving toward becoming energy self-sufficient by pumping natural gas from offshore fields in the Mediterranean.

CHAPTER 6
The Environment

Lake Kinneret, the Jordan River, and the Dead Sea straddle the Great Rift Valley—a tear in the Earth stretching from Turkey in the north to deep into Africa in the south. With enormous pressure, two tectonic plates grind away at each other as they move slowly in opposite directions. Tremors and small earthquakes occur regularly as the plates slip. Every century or so in recorded history there has been an earthquake powerful enough to have resulted in human death and widespread property damage. The last big one was on July 11, 1927. An earthquake with its epicenter located in the northern Dead Sea—believed by seismologists today to have had a magnitude of 6.3 on the Richter Scale[1]—struck what was then the British Mandate of Palestine, causing widespread damage in Jerusalem, Nablus, Jericho, and Tiberias. An estimated 268 people were killed.[2]

If Mother Nature can be cruel here with droughts and earthquakes, man too has been a terrible custodian of the earth. Oak forests were part of the Biblical landscape and small sections remained into the nineteenth century, explains tree expert Yaacov Shkolnik.[3] He recalls how King David's rebellious son Absalom was caught by his curly hair in the branches of a large oak in the forests of Gilead while the mule he was riding kept on going.[4] Today trees of that stature are rare.

Where did the forests disappear to? Wars, overgrazing by Bedouins' flocks of black goats, the production of whitewash to protect adobe (mud brick) houses, and wood-burning railroad locomotives all contributed to the denuding of the landscape.

Amongst the objectives of Zionism was to reverse this environmental degradation—to make the desert bloom. Forestation, ecology, conservation, and biodiversity were major issues in Israel decades before they became buzzwords in the West.

The Jewish National Fund has planted 250 million trees since it was founded in 1901,[5] making Israel the only country in the world with more trees in 2000 than it had a century earlier.[6] More than 70 percent of Israelis have personally planted trees,[7] and Arbor Day when the almond trees blossom pink is a holiday. Many tourists include planting a sapling in their itinerary.

On Arbor Day, called *Tu B'Shvat* in Hebrew, hundreds of thousands of school children plant saplings as part of Israel's national afforestation project. More than 250 million trees have been planted since 1901, greening former deserts and denuded landscapes.

NO CAROB, SABRA, OR
ORANGE TREES IN THE BIBLE

Picking up a carob pod to munch on, Yaakov Shkolnik notes that while one hundred species of plants and trees are mentioned in the Hebrew Bible, including the seven species—wheat, barley, grapes, figs, pomegranates, olives, and dates—the carob is not one of them.[8] Yet the carob tree features prominently in the Mishna written down some five hundred years later. Shkolnik cites the story of Rabbi Shimon Bar Yohai and his son Eleazar who for twelve years hid from the Romans in the Galilee village of Peki'in, nourished only by a carob tree and a spring. A similar legend exists about John the Baptist subsisting on the slightly sweet pods in the wilderness, hence their nickname: St. John's bread.

"It's very odd that it's not mentioned in the Bible but then suddenly becomes widespread," says Shkolnik.[9] Similarly two of Israel's botanic icons—the orange tree and the sabra cactus—are not indigenous. They were brought to the Mediterranean basin, from China and Mexico respectively. Today the sabra pear is said to be like native-born Israelis—prickly on the surface but sweet inside.

"One theory is the carob tree was introduced into the Land of Israel after the Bible ended, and then spread across the Near East," concludes Shkolnik. "It's one of the mysteries of the Bible."[10]

Carob pods

Ostriches are just one of many species that roamed Israel in Biblical times, but later became extinct in the land. Hunting and the destruction of habitat caused many of these regional extinctions. Today these animals are being reintroduced at the Yotvata Hai-Bar Nature Reserve in the Arava Desert.

CHAPTER 7
Birds, Beasts, and the Bible

American humorist Mark Twain visited the Holy Land in 1867. Two years later in his travelogue *The Innocents Abroad*, he described the country—covered with lush forest in the time of the Bible—as a ruin:

> Of all the lands there are for dismal scenery, I think Palestine must be the prince. The hills are barren, they are dull of color, they are unpicturesque in shape. The valleys are unsightly deserts fringed with a feeble vegetation that has an expression about it of being sorrowful and **despondent**. The Dead Sea and the Sea of Galilee sleep in the midst of a vast stretch of hill and plain wherein the eye rests upon no pleasant tint, no striking object, no soft picture dreaming in a purple haze or **mottled** with the shadows of the clouds. Every outline is harsh, every feature is distinct, there is no perspective—distance works no enchantment here. It is a hopeless, dreary, heart-broken land.[1]

As Israel's forests were cut down, the fauna lost their habitat. Species were hunted to extinction. There are no more crocodiles in the Crocodile River. The lion of Judah may grace Jerusalem's municipal emblem, but no more prides of lions roam the country as they did in the time of the Biblical strongman

Samson, or when David the shepherd fought off a big cat trying to snatch one of his sheep.

The Zionist movement has aimed to restore the land and reverse habitat destruction, reintroducing the wildlife that once roamed here. The Yotvata Hai-Bar Nature Reserve in the Arava Desert is part of that initiative. Here at a three-thousand-acre ranch run by the Israel Nature and Parks Authority, endangered and locally extinct animals mentioned in the Bible are bred in the hope of reintroducing them in the desert. So far the Asian wild ass (or onager) has already been released to roam wild in the Makhtesh Ramon crater. Bring your camera and zoom lens to shoot the ostrich, gazelle, caracal, and other rare desert animals. Keep in mind that the fauna in the desert is largely nocturnal. At noon most animals are sleeping in the shade.

Caracal

So successful has the Hai-Bar desert breeding program been that a second ranch was established aiming to reintroduce the fauna of Mediterranean forest. The Carmel Hai-Bar Nature Reserve stretches across 1,500 acres on Mount Carmel near Haifa in the north. Here you'll discover Persian fallow deer and white-tailed eagles.

Apart from the twin Hai-Bar reserves, and thanks to strict gun control, Israel does have some notable wildlife. A herd of gazelles graze in a park in Jerusalem. Desert foxes prowl the roads in the still of the night. But the best place to shoot big game with your camera is Ein Gedi—an oasis with a series of dramatic waterfalls

One of the waterfalls at
the Ein Gedi oasis

near the Dead Sea. Here the ibex wait patiently for the national park to close so they can come to drink the cool water. Rock hyraxes sun themselves, oblivious to hikers. Alas leopards are now extinct here.

It's to the skies however that one must look to appreciate Israel's wildlife: to the delight of birdwatchers, the tiny country is a feathered superpower.

At least five hundred million birds—including pelicans, cranes, storks, falcons, eagles, sparrows, common redshanks, and warblers—wing their way across Israel's skies twice a year during the migration seasons.[2] In the fall, they make their way south to Central Africa and in the spring they return to Europe to mate.

Israel owes its remarkable variety of birds to geography: flying thousands of miles in weeks, the migrating birds need to stop to rest. To Israel's east, the Syrian Desert offers little food or water; to the west the Mediterranean Sea has few islands on which to land. The Hula Valley in Israel's north has the perfect blend of land, water, and nutrition.

And to the fascination of professional and amateur **ornithologists**, the best bird-watching site of all is the Agamon-Hula Preserve near the Galilee Panhandle city of Kiryat Shmona. The peak time to visit Agamon-Hula is October through December. The birds begin returning north from Africa in late February. The best way to see the Agamon-Hula feeding area is by traveling along the reserve's 5.3-mile- (8.6-kilometer-) long trail with a bicycle or electric golf cart.

Apart from the Agamon-Hula, Israel offers bird lovers a series of bird-watching sites stretching along the north-south migration route. These include the Beit Shean Valley's Kfar Ruppin, Neve Eitan, Maoz Hayim, and Tirat Zevi. All of these locations have major concentrations of fishponds—in other words, lunch for raptors.

Further to the south in the Arava Desert, the birding center at Kibbutz Lotan is also a favorite spot. One only needs to look up to see the sky full of eagles, storks, or pelicans. At Ein Evrona just north of Eilat, a flock of wild flamingoes are tickled pink not to have to migrate between Turkey and Africa anymore, having found lots of food at the local saltwater fish ponds.

The most important of Israel's several bird research centers is Tel Aviv University's International Center for the Study of Bird Migration at Latrun. The center uses cameras, radar, and satellites to track the flocks, and updates the birds' movements on its website. That data is also invaluable for minimizing potentially deadly encounters between birds and airplanes.

THE DEAD SEA IS NOT DYING

The Dead can't be dying; it's already dead. At 1,404 feet (428 meters) below sea level, and dropping three feet (one meter) per year, the Dead Sea is the lowest place on the face of the Earth. Some scientists have suggested that the salt lake is suffering irreversible environmental damage—that the Dead Sea is dying. They say this is because people in the area have been using increasing amounts of water for agriculture and mining the lake for minerals.

With the water's 33.7 percent salinity, the Dead Sea can't support life other than microbes. That hyper-salinity attracts bathers to experience floating with both hands and feet out of the water. Nevertheless the Dead Sea isn't the place you'll learn to swim. If the salt gets in your eyes you'll want to wash them immediately. Any cut on your skin will sting.

Floating in the Dead Sea

Salt deposits on the shoreline

While in 2012 the World Bank funded a study to examine building a 120-mile- (193-kilometer-) long canal between the Red Sea and the Dead Sea, scientists oppose this idea. On the positive side, such a huge engineering project would produce vast amounts of desalinated water for parched Jordan, and would halt the shrinking of the Dead Sea. On the negative side, however, the project could cause devastating environmental damage. A better solution, say scientists like Professor Zvi Ben Avraham of Tel Aviv University, would be to open the dams that prevent the Jordan and Yarmuk Rivers from flowing south into the Dead Sea.

What if nothing is done? The Dead Sea will never entirely dry up, Ben Avraham responds. While the southern section is already an artificial lake held behind earth dams, the northern half will continue to subside a further 300 feet (91 meters). At that point, which he predicts will arrive in approximately two centuries, the even more saline water will achieve a new equilibrium between winter rain runoff and evaporation.

Camels are called the "ships of the desert." When you ride one, you'll understand why. The wadis and canyons near Eilat provide the setting for many camel safaris.

CHAPTER 8
Eilat Beckons with Desert Adventure

Besides the usual sun, sea, and sports attractions, the all-but-rainless Red Sea resort of Eilat offers adventures and experiences for practically every age, taste, and budget.

Ever wanted to swim with dolphins? Flipper awaits you at the Dolphin Reef where a school of bottlenose dolphins—including babies born at the site—maintain their daily routine of hunting, playing, and courting. The highly sociable marine mammals are free to choose between human company or continuing their daily routine in the school. Visitors who are comfortable in the ocean can join a guided swim or dive. Those who prefer not to get wet can watch the frolicking from dockside.

While camels may not be nearly as cute or communicative as dolphins, a ride on the "ship of the desert" is an unforgettable experience. Camel safaris range from a few hours to two days. Traveling through a *wadi* (dry riverbed) at night, especially under a full moon, you're likely to encounter the nocturnal rodents, raptors, and lizards that transform the seemingly barren desert into a place teeming with life.

While riding camels through desert canyons appeals to some, to really appreciate the desert's harsh yet beautiful landscape and its unique flora and fauna, you're going to have to slow down and put on your hiking boots. The Eilat Mountains Nature Reserve offers fabulous hiking trails of varying difficulty. These trails require good orienteering skills. Detailed maps in

Eilat's year-round warm temperatures have made it a popular resort for European vacationers, as well as Tel Avivis who fly down for the weekend.

The Dolphin Reef lets visitors get up close and personal with the family of bottlenose dolphins who live there.

The water of the Gulf of Eilat remains above 70 degrees Fahrenheit (21 degrees Celsius) even in the winter—an ideal temperature for tropical coral reefs.

A scuba diver's view of coral reef and fish

English are available from the Society for the Protection of Nature at the Eilat Field School. The rangers' recommendations are free.

In the Uvda Valley north of Eilat you'll encounter a mysterious nine-thousand-year-old Neolithic temple dedicated to hunting the rare leopard. Just south of the temple are Sahara-like sand dunes—perfect for running, sliding, or rolling down to burn off some pent up energy.

A short 19-mile (30-kilometer) drive north of Eilat is Timna Park—a geological and archaeological wonderland including copper mines from the time of the Egyptian Pharaohs. Don't miss Solomon's Pillars—a natural sandstone formation where the ancient Egyptian miners built a shrine to their goddess Hathor. While the temple is ruined, the image of the goddess is visible where it was carved on a cliff.

In stark contrast to the Copper Age ruins, a fifty-megawatt solar energy park is now under construction at Timna. Together with similar sun electricity projects nearby, the Timna solar field will supply all of Eilat's power.[1]

עמודי שלמה
SOLOMON'S PILLARS

FISHY BUSINESS

Tired of the drab desert? Grab your snorkel and fins to see the neon fish that make their home in the world's most northern tropical coral reef. And then check out the ships that were sunk to provide the foundation for an artificial reef. The Coral Reserve includes the Underwater Observatory—a building where one descends below the waves outside to observe the reef life and fish through glass windows.

Underwater Observatory

If you're adamant about not getting your feet wet in the Red Sea's wonderfully warm waters, another alternative is the glass-bottom boats which offer a gander at the iridescent fish. Which brings us back to the beachfront pedestrian promenade connecting many of Eilat's hotels.

If you're keen to swap Eilat's 100-degree-Fahrenheit (40-degree-Celsius) summer heat for an Alaska-like January day, check out the Ice Space bar—an igloo made from 150 tons (136 metric tons) of ice. Warm clothes are provided and your chilled drinks are served in ice cups. The temperature is kept at 14 degrees Fahrenheit (-10 degrees Celsius)—cool enough to maintain the frozen fixtures and fittings, while not giving frostbite to the tourists who come by for a cool experience. In the same spirit, you'll find a skating rink nearby in the hotel district.

My personal favorite site in Eilat is the monument on the beach depicting the flag raising of March 1949. This event marked the end of Israel's War of Independence. Among the liberators was my father-in-law Israel Turkienicz, a Holocaust survivor who came to Palestine and joined the pre-state Palmach underground army.

Thanks Issy! The next time I'm at the Ice Space bar, I'll raise my frosted glass of beer to you. It's due to you and your brave comrades-in-arms that today in Eilat life is a beach and I'm chillin'.

UNESCO'S WORLD HERITAGE LIST PROJECT

Work with a partner, or divide into two groups of students. Review UNESCO's World Heritage List selection criteria here:

http://whc.unesco.org/en/criteria/

Each person or group should research key synagogues, churches, mosques, shrines, or archaeological and historic sites in the Old City of Jerusalem and its surrounding hills Mount Zion and the Mount of Olives, and choose one that meets one of the criteria for selection. Write a report in which you explain why your site should be chosen for inclusion on the World Heritage List.

Review your partner's or the other team's report and respond to the report as the UNESCO World Heritage Committee. Decide whether to include the site on the list or not, and explain your position.

The Mount of Olives

The Church of All Nations

Ramban Synagogue

TIMELINE

BCE

ca. 1700	Abraham buys a double cave in Hebron and buries his wife Sarah there.
ca. 1010	King David captures Canaanite Jerusalem. He renames it the City of David, and makes it the capital of the United Kingdom of Israel.
ca. 960	King Solomon builds the First Holy Temple in Jerusalem.
ca. 800	King Hezekiah digs his water diversion project called Hezekiah's Tunnel.
586	Babylonian emperor Nebuchadnezzar destroys the Holy Temple and exiles the Jewish People to today's Iraq.
ca. 538	Zerubbabel leads the return of the first group of Jewish exiles and subsequently builds the Second Holy Temple.
ca. 74	Birth of King Herod.
63	Rome occupies Judea.
ca. 4	Jesus of Nazareth is born.

CE

26	Pontius Pilate becomes Roman governor of Judea.
ca. 33	Crucifixion of Jesus.
ca. 57	Paul imprisoned in Caesarea.
66	Beginning of the Jewish Revolt against Rome.
70	Titus destroys Jerusalem and the Second Holy Temple.
73	The rebels at Masada commit suicide rather than surrender to Rome.
637	Omar captures Jerusalem, beginning the Arab period.
691	Dome of the Rock completed.
1265	Mamluk Sultan Baybars captures Caesarea.
1291	The last Crusaders are driven from the Holy Land. The Mamluks burn down the Crusaders' deserted castles and cities.
1581	German cartographer Heinrich Bünting depicts Jerusalem as a clover leaf uniting Europe, Africa, and Asia.
1867	American humorist Mark Twain visits Israel. Two years later he publishes his bestselling travelogue *The Innocents Abroad*.
1878	Petach Tikvah, Israel's first modern agricultural settlement, established.
1882	First Aliyah, wave of Jewish immigration to Israel, begins.
1892	Jaffa-Jerusalem Railroad inaugurated, the first in the Middle East.
1901	Jewish National Fund founded to purchase land for a Jewish state.
1909	Tel Aviv founded.
1922	The League of Nations approves a mandate giving Britain the authority to administer Palestine (modern Israel).
1927	6.3 Richter earthquake devastates Israel.
1939	World War II begins.
1947	First Dead Sea Scrolls discovered; Israel's War of Independence begins, called *al-Nakba* (the Disaster) by Palestinians.
1948	The State is Israel is declared.
1964	Israel inaugurates the National Water Carrier.
1986	"Jesus Boat" discovered at Kibbutz Ginosar.
1995	Prime Minister Yitzhak Rabin assassinated at a Tel Aviv peace rally.
1999	Israel signs the World Heritage Convention.
2014	Beit Guvrin-Maresha Caves National Park is added to the UNESCO World Heritage list, bringing the total number of Israeli sites on the list to eight.
2015	Prime Minister Benjamin Netanyahu is returned to office, and forms a new coalition government.

CHAPTER NOTES

Chapter 1: Jerusalem's Old City

1. Estimate for year-end 2015 is 40,707, based on a year-end 2012 population of 38,700 and an average annual growth rate of 1.7 percent. Old City growth rate and population data are from: Dr. Maya Chosen, ed., *Statistical Yearbook of Jerusalem*, no. 28—2014 (Jerusalem: The Jerusalem Institute for Israel Studies, 2014), pp. 58, 95, http://www.jiis.org.il/.upload/yearbook2014/shnaton_part1.pdf

2. Quran 17:1, in *The Holy Qur'an: Text, Translation, and Commentary, translated by Abdullah Yusuf Ali* (Washington, DC: The Islamic Center, 1978).

3. 2 Samuel 5:6 (New English Bible).

4. Jerome Murphy-O'Connor, *The Holy Land: An Archaeological Guide from Earliest Times to 1700* (Oxford: Oxford University Press, 1980), p. 80.

Chapter 2: New Jerusalem

1. Estimate for year-end 2015 is 816,884, based on a year-end 2012 population of 815,300 and an average annual growth rate of 1.7 percent, minus Jerusalem's Old City population estimate of 40,707. Growth rate and population data are from: Dr. Maya Chosen, ed., *Statistical Yearbook of Jerusalem*, no. 28—2014 (Jerusalem: The Jerusalem Institute for Israel Studies, 2014), pp. 56, 58, http://www.jiis.org.il/.upload/yearbook2014/shnaton_part1.pdf

2. Yad Vashem, "Names and Numbers of Righteous Among the Nations—Per Country & Ethnic Origin, as of January 1, 2014," http://www.yadvashem.org/yv/en/righteous/statistics.asp

3. Sulaiman Abu Zayad (grave digger at the Franciscan Cemetery on Mount Zion), interview with the author, February 1993.

Chapter 3: Show and Tel—The Big Orange is Israel's Business Heart

1. Estimate for year-end 2015 is 427,014, based on a year-end 2013 population of 418,600 and an average annual growth rate of 1 percent. Data is from: Central Bureau of Statistics, *Statistical Abstract of Israel 2014*, No. 65, "Sources of Population Growth, by Type of Locality, Population Group and Religion," http://www.cbs.gov.il/reader/shnaton/templ_shnaton_e.html?num_tab=st02_14&CYear=2014

2. Ezekiel 3:15 (New English Bible).

Chapter 4: Lake Kinneret and the Galilee

1. Mark 6:30-44 (New English Bible).

2. Matthew 5:5 (New English Bible).

3. Israel Water Authority, "The Sea of Galilee," January 1, 2014, http://147.237.72.10/water/watec/003_Kinert-Small.wmv

4. Bet Alon Museum, "Boat Discovery," http://www.bet-alon.co.il/museum/content.php?page_id=60

5. Shelley Wachsmann, *The Sea of Galilee Boat* (New York: Perseus Publishing, 2000), p. 249.

CHAPTER NOTES

Chapter 5: Caesarea—Cutting Edge Water Technology

1. Kenneth G. Holum, Robert L. Hohlfelder, Robert J. Bull, and Avner Raban, *King Herod's Dream: Caesarea on the Sea* (New York: W. W. Norton & Company, 1988), pp. 72–73.

2. Acts 24:1-27 (New English Bible).

3. Holum, *King Herod's Dream*, p. 237.

4. Eduard G. Reinhardt, et al., "The Tsunami of 13 December A.D. 115 and the Destruction of Herod the Great's Harbor at Caesarea Maritima, Israel," *Geology*, v. 34, no. 12, July 3, 2006, pp. 1061–1064, http://geology.gsapubs.org/content/34/12/1061.abstract

5. Joseph Francois Michaud, *The History of the Crusades*, Vol. 3, trans. William Robson (New York: A. C. Armstrong & Son, 1881), p. 70.

6. Ma'aan-Michael Agro Center: The Agro-Powerhouse, "About/History," http://maaganagro.bsmart.co.il/HTMLs/article.aspx?C2004=12026&BSP=12020

7. Ibid.

8. Kibbutzim Site, "The Kibbutz Movement—Facts and Figures," http://www.kibbutz.org.il/eng/

Chapter 6: The Environment

1. National Geophysical Data Center/World Data Service, "Significant Earthquake Database," http://www.ngdc.noaa.gov/nndc/struts/form?t=101650&s=1&d=1

2. Ibid.

3. Yaacov Shkolnik (Israeli arborist), tour attended by the author, January 7, 2010.

4. 2 Samuel 18:9 (New English Bible).

5. Jewish National Fund, "Tree Planting Center," http://www.jnf.org/support/tree-planting-center/

6. Yaacov Shkolnik (Israeli arborist), tour attended by the author, January 7, 2010.

7. Ibid.

8. Deuteronomy 8:8 (New English Bible); and Yaacov Shkolnik (Israeli arborist), tour attended by the author, January 7, 2010.

9. Yaacov Shkolnik (Israeli arborist), tour attended by the author, January 7, 2010.

10. Ibid.

Chapter 7: Birds, Beasts, and the Bible

1. Mark Twain, *The Innocents Abroad* (New York: Signet Classics, 1966), p. 473.

2. Israeli Birding Website, http://www.israbirding.com/

Chapter 8: Eilat Beckons with Desert Adventure

1. Karen Kloosterman, "New 50MW Solar Park Near Israel's Timna Copper Mines Seeks Partners," *Green Prophet*, September 9, 2014, http://www.greenprophet.com/2014/09/solar-energy-timna-park/

WORKS CONSULTED

Abu Zayad, Sulaiman (grave digger at the Franciscan Cemetery on Mount Zion). Interview with the author, February 1993.

Ali, Abdullah Yusuf. *The Holy Qur'an: Text, Translation, and Commentary*. Washington, DC: The Islamic Center, 1978.

Bet Alon Museum. "Boat Discovery." http://www.bet-alon.co.il/museum/content.php?page_id=60

Central Bureau of Statistics. *Statistical Abstract of Israel 2014*, No. 65. "Sources of Population Growth, by Type of Locality, Population Group and Religion." http://www.cbs.gov.il/reader/shnaton/templ_shnaton_e.html?num_tab=st02_14&CYear=2014

Chosen, Dr. Maya., ed. *Statistical Yearbook of Jerusalem*, no. 28—2014. Jerusalem: The Jerusalem Institute for Israel Studies, 2014. http://www.jiis.org.il/.upload/yearbook2014/shnaton_part1.pdf

Comay, Joan, and Ronald Brownrigg. *Who's Who in the Bible: The Old Testament and the Apocrypha, The New Testament*. New York: Wing Books, 1993.

Crown-Tamir, Hela. *How to Walk in the Footsteps of Jesus and the Prophets: A Scripture Reference Guide for Biblical Sites in Israel and Jordan*. Jerusalem: Gefen, 2000.

Dintaman, Anna, and David Landis. *Hiking the Jesus Trail and Other Biblical Walks in the Galilee*. Harleysville, PA: Village to Village Press, 2013.

Finkelstein, Israel, and Amihai Mazar. *The Quest for the Historical Israel: Debating Archaeology and the History of Early Israel*. Atlanta: Society of Biblical Literature, 2007.

Holum, Kenneth G., Robert L. Hohlfelder, Robert J. Bull, and Avner Raban. *King Herod's Dream: Caesarea on the Sea*. New York: W. W. Norton & Company, 1988.

Israeli Birding Website. http://www.israbirding.com/

Israel Water Authority. "The Sea of Galilee." January 1, 2014. http://147.237.72.10/water/watec/003_Kinert-Small.wmv

Jewish National Fund. "Tree Planting Center." http://www.jnf.org/support/tree-planting-center/

Kibbutzim Site. "The Kibbutz Movement—Facts and Figures." http://www.kibbutz.org.il/eng/

Kloosterman, Karen. "New 50MW Solar Park Near Israel's Timna Copper Mines Seeks Partners." *Green Prophet*, September 9, 2014. http://www.greenprophet.com/2014/09/solar-energy-timna-park/

Laqueur, Walter. *A History of Zionism: From the French Revolution to the Establishment of the State of Israel*. New York: Knopf Doubleday, 2004.

Ma'agan-Michael Agro Center: The Agro-Powerhouse. "About/History." http://maaganagro.bsmart.co.il/HTMLs/article.aspx?C2004=12026&BSP=12020

Mekorot Israel National Water Company. "The Water Level of the Kinneret." http://www.mekorot.co.il/Eng/newsite/InformationCenter/Pages/WaterLevelKinneret.aspx

Michaud, Joseph Francois. *The History of the Crusades*, Vol. 3. Translated by William Robson. New York: A. C. Armstrong & Son, 1881.

Montefiore, Simon Sebag. *Jerusalem: The Biography*. London: Weidenfeld & Nicolson, 2011.

Murphy-O'Connor, Jerome. *The Holy Land: An Archaeological Guide from Earliest Times to 1700*. Oxford: Oxford University Press, 1980.

Naor, Dr. Mordechai. "Tel-Aviv Centennial—'Ahuzat-Bayit' Land Lottery." *Boeliem*, June 20, 2008. http://51706862.nl.strato-hosting.eu/content/2008/792.html

National Geophysical Data Center/World Data Service. "Significant Earthquake Database." http://www.ngdc.noaa.gov/nndc/struts/form?t=101650&s=1&d=1

The New English Bible. Cambridge: Cambridge University Press, 1972.

Reinhardt, Eduard G., Beverly N. Goodman, Joe I. Boyce, Gloria Lopez, Peter van Hengstum, W. Jack Rink, Yossi Mart, and Avner Raban. "The Tsunami of 13 December A.D. 115 and the Destruction of Herod the Great's Harbor at Caesarea Maritima, Israel." *Geology*, v. 34, no. 12, July 3, 2006. pp. 1061-1064. http://geology.gsapubs.org/content/34/12/1061.abstract

WORKS CONSULTED

Roller, Duane W. *The Building Program of Herod the Great*. Berkeley, CA: University of California Press, 1998.

Segev, Tom. *One Palestine, Complete: Jews and Arabs under the British Mandate*. New York: Metropolitan Books, 2000.

Senor, Dan, and Saul Singer. *Start-Up Nation: The Story of Israel's Economic Miracle*. New York: Twelve, 2009.

Shavit, Ari. *My Promised Land: The Triumph and Tragedy of Israel*. New York: Spiegel & Grau, 2013.

Shkolnik, Yaacov (Israeli arborist). Tour attended by the author, January 7, 2010.

Silberman, Neil Asher. *Digging for God and Country: Exploration, Archeology and the Secret Struggle for the Holy Land, 1799–1917*. New York: Alfred A. Knopf, 1982.

Stanford University. "Ahuzat Bayit and the Founding of Tel Aviv in 1909." The Eliasaf Robinson Tel Aviv Collection. https://lib.stanford.edu/eliasaf-robinson-tel-aviv-collection/ahuzat-bayit-and-founding-tel-aviv-1909

Twain, Mark. *The Innocents Abroad*. New York: Signet Classics, 1966.

Wachsmann, Shelley. *The Sea of Galilee Boat: A 2000 Year Old Discovery from the Sea of Legends*. New York: Perseus Publishing, 2000.

Weill-Rochant, Catherine. "Myths and Buildings of Tel Aviv." *Bulletin du Centre de Recherche Français à Jérusalem*, December 2003, pp. 152–63. http://bcrfj.revues.org/672

Willis, Bailey. "Earthquakes in the Holy Land." *Bulletin of the Seismological Society of America*, v. 18, June 1928.

Yad Vashem. "Names and Numbers of Righteous Among the Nations—Per Country & Ethnic Origin, as of January 1, 2014." http://www.yadvashem.org/yv/en/righteous/statistics.asp

FURTHER READING

Fegelman, Richard, Victoria Liu, and Alexander Traub. *Let's Go Israel: The Student Travel Guide*. Cambridge, MA: Harvard Student Agencies, 2011.

Frank, Mitch. *Understanding the Holy Land*. New York: Viking, 2005.

Rivlin, Lily. *Welcome to Israel!* Springfield, NJ: Behrman House, 2000.

Yomtov, Nel. *Enchantment of the World: Israel*. New York: Children's Press, 2012.

ON THE INTERNET

City of David, Ancient Jerusalem
http://www.cityofdavid.org.il/en

Dolphin Reef Eilat
http://www.dolphinreef.co.il/

International Center for the Study of Bird Migration
http://www.birds.org.il/en/index.aspx

Israel Ministry of Tourism
http://www.goisrael.com/tourism_eng/Pages/home.aspx

The Israel Museum
http://www.english.imjnet.org.il/

Society for the Preservation of Israel Heritage Sites (SPIHS)
http://eng.shimur.org/

United Nations Educational, Scientific and Cultural Organization: World Heritage Convention. "Israel."
http://whc.unesco.org/en/statesparties/IL/

Yad VaShem
http://www.yadvashem.org/

GLOSSARY

agro-industrial (AG-roh-in-DUH-stree-uhl)—farming on a large scale using modern technology and equipment

archaeologist (ahr-kee-OL-uh-jist)—a person who studies prehistoric humans by examining the artifacts they left behind

chutzpah (KHOOT-spuh)—nerve

civil engineering—the design and construction of roads, bridges, harbors, canals, dams, etc.

despondent (dih-SPON-duhnt)—showing or feeling hopelessness

explicitly (ik-SPLIS-it-lee)—clearly

incense (IN-sens)—a substance that produces a pleasant smell when burned

Ka'aba (KAH-uh-buh)—a small, cubical building in the courtyard of the Great Mosque at Mecca containing a sacred black stone

kibbutz (KI-boots)—a collective settlement in Israel

lingua franca (LING-gwuh FRANG-kuh)—main language

matriarch (MEY-tree-ahrk)—female head of a tribal line

mausoleum (maw-suh-LEE-uhm)—a large, impressive tomb, usually in the form of a building

mottled (MOT-ld)—discolored with blotches or spots

Nabatean (nab-uh-TEE-uhn)—related to the ancient Arab Nabatean kingdom, which existed from the second century BCE until the second century CE

ornithologist (awr-nuh-THOL-uh-jist)—a scientist who studies birds

pagan (PEY-guhn)—related to a religion or belief system that is not Islam, Christianity, or Judaism

patriarch (PEY-tree-ahrk)—male head of a tribal line

ramparts (RAM-pahrts)—walls that are built around a place as protection

secular (SEK-yuh-ler)—not connected with religion

synagogue (SIN-uh-gawg)—a Jewish house of worship

utopian commune (yoo-TOH-pee-uhn)—a group of people living together as a community, with a lifestyle and government that the group believes is perfect

PHOTO CREDITS: Design elements from Thinkstock and Dreamstime/Sharon Beck. Cover, pp. 2–3, 4–5, 10–11 (background), 11 (front), 12, 17 (background, top front), 20, 23, 26 (top), 28, 30–31 (background) 36–37 (background), 36 (front), 39, 40, 43, 46, 48, 49, 52–53 (background), 56—Thinkstock; p. 2 (map)—United Naiions; p. 8 (top front, left)—Rostislav Glinksy/Dreamstime; p. 8 (top front, right, background), 17 (front, bottom), 32, 42—Lucidwaters/Dreamstime; pp. 4, 8 (front, bottom), 10 (front), 13, 14 (background), 50, 64—Gil Zohar; p. 14 (inset)—Little Savage/Public Domain; pp. 17, 31 (statue), 37 (front), 49 (front)—Barbara Mitchell; p. 18—public domain; p. 19—Joris Van Ostaeyen/Dreamstime; p. 22—Government Press Office/Saar Yaacov; p.24—Sambach/cc-by-sa; p. 26—Avishai Teicher/public domain; p. 33—Ministry of Tourism/Government of Israel; p. 34—Pavel Bernshtam/Dreamstime; p. 44—Gorshkov13/Dreamstime; p. 47—Konstantin32/Dreamstime; pp. 52 (front), 55—Dafna Tal/Ministry of Tourism/Government of Israel; p. 54—Gavril Margittai/Dreamstime; p. 56—Ido Winter/CC0 1.0 Universal public domain.

INDEX

About the Author

Gil Zohar was born in Toronto, Canada, and moved to Jerusalem in 1982. He is a journalist writing for *The Jerusalem Post*, *Segula* magazine, and other publications. As well, he's a professional tour guide who likes to weave together the Holy Land's multiple narratives. Gil wrote one hundred pages of *Fodor's Guide to Israel* (7th edition, 2009) and has written tourism promotion material for Israel's Ministry of Tourism. He can be reached at GilZohar@rogers.com or +011 972 (0)524 817 482. For more information see www.GilZohar.ca.

מועצה אזורית
תמר

צאתכם לשלום
Go in Peace
رافقتكم السلامة